THE DARK PHILOSOPHERS

Based on the life and stories of Gwyn Thomas
Adapted by Carl Grose and the company

First performed on 11th November 2010
at the Riverfront Theatre & Arts Centre, Newport.
Restaged at the Traverse Theatre August 9th-28th 2011.

NATIONAL
THEATRE --- ---- WALES

Told by an Idiot

TRAVERSE
THEATRE

A letter from Gwyn Thomas to the Producers of *James Bond*.

Dear Mr Saltzman, Dear Mr Broccoli,

I hear you are looking for a new James Bond and you suggest a younger man. I think this is a mistake. You need an older man and I think I fit the bill. I am sixty-six. I am still an effective lover and a pretty handy tenor with an extraordinary ear. If ever you should get James Bond to sing, and it's about time that he did for a change, I'm your man.

I notice that you want a man who walks well. You say he should move like Robert Mitchum, Gary Cooper, Clark Gable. I haven't actually seen these men in action and have no idea what is special in the way they walked as I only went to the cinema once when I was on the rota of voluntary ushers at the Welfare Hall. However, I think I walk all right. I live on a hill riddled with ruts and pot-holes and have grown very agile over the years, dodging these traps. This would come in useful for me when I have to fling myself flat at the approach of bullets.

I think I should mention that I tend to walk in a rather low-slung sort of way. I asked Alderman Beynon if he thought this would spoil my chances as a successor to Sean Connery. He said no, like a shot!

Yours sincerely
Gwyn Thomas

The Dark Philosophers was commissioned and produced by National Theatre Wales in partnership with Told by an Idiot on 11th November 2010 at the Riverfront in Newport as part of National Theatre Wales' launch year.

The production was restaged for the Edinburgh Festival Fringe 2011 with the following cast and creative team:

Cast
David Charles
Nia Davies
Nia Gwynne
Ryan Hacker
Daniel Hawksford
Bettrys Jones
Matthew Owen
Glyn Pritchard

Creative Team
Writer, **Carl Grose**
Director, **Paul Hunter**
Designer, **Angela Davies**
Lighting Designer, **Ceri James**
Music Composed and Directed by **Iain Johnstone**
Sound Designer, **Laura Coates**

Production Manager, **Matt Noddings**
Company Stage Manager, **Richard Walker**
Deputy Stage Manager, **Carol Pestridge**
Assistant Stage Manager, **Cordelia Ashwell**
Assistant Stage Manager, **Kelsi Lewis**
Costume Supervisor, **Angharad Matthews**

Cyngor Celfyddydau Cymru
Arts Council of Wales

Noddir gan
Lywodraeth Cymru
Sponsored by
Welsh Government

Supported by
ARTS COUNCIL
ENGLAND

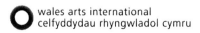

wales arts international
celfyddydau rhyngwladol cymru

BRITISH
COUNCIL

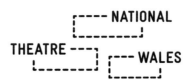
NATIONAL THEATRE WALES

National Theatre Wales was launched in November 2009, and creates invigorating theatre in the English language, rooted in Wales, with an international reach. It is Wales' first English-language national theatre company.

The curtain was raised on its first production in March 2010 for a launch year of 13 productions in 13 months, one per month, in locations across the country, alongside an innovative programme of community events and digital activity.

Productions include: *A Good Night Out in the Valleys*; *The Devil Inside Him*; *The Beach*; *The Persians* (Winner of the TMA Award for Best Design and the Ted Hughes Award for Poetry); *The Weather Factory*; and *The Passion* ("one of the outstanding theatrical events not only of this year, but of the decade" *The Observer*).

National Theatre Wales is supported by Arts Council of Wales and the Welsh Government.

> "The big success story [of 2010] was the foundation of National Theatre Wales" – **Michael Billington**

National Theatre Wales
30 Castle Arcade
Cardiff / CF10 1BW

Phone +44 (0)29 2035 3070
info@nationaltheatrewales.org
nationaltheatrewales.org

Twitter: @ntwtweets
To Keep up-to-date with the latest information, text NTW Y2 to 61211.

Told by an Idiot

Told by an Idiot was founded in 1993 by Hayley Carmichael, Paul Hunter and John Wright and has built a reputation for producing work that is moving, comic and utterly theatrical. Revelling in a style of theatre that is bigger than life, the company sets out to discover the epic in the most personal of stories, whilst treading a fine line between comedy and tragedy. Acknowledging the artifice of theatre, the company make no attempt to put reality on stage, but remain, however, fascinated by the fine line between comedy and tragedy that exists in the real world. Through collaborating, devising and a playful but rigorous approach to text, the company aims to tell stories using a wealth of imagery and a rich theatrical language, creating a genuinely spontaneous experience for the audience which is accessible to all.

Told by an Idiot has performed throughout the world, working with celebrated artists including Richard Wilson O.B.E., Carol Ann Duffy, Philip Pullman and Michel Faber.

Productions include: *And The Horse You Rode In On; The Comedy Of Errors; The Dark Philosophers; The Fahrenheit Twins; Casanova* (with poet laureate Carol Ann Duffy); *The Firework-Maker's Daughter; I'm A Fool To Want You; Playing The Victim; A Little Fantasy; Aladdin; I Can't Wake Up; Shoot Me In The Heart* (nominated for Manchester Evening News award) *Happy Birthday Mr Deka D; I Weep At My Piano* (winner of Time Out Live award) *Don't Laugh It's My Life; You Haven't Embraced Me Yet; I'm So Big; On The Verge Of Exploding*.

For further information or to join our mailing list, please contact us at:

Told by an Idiot
Unit LF 1.7
The Leathermarket, Weston Street
London SE1 3ER

020 7407 4123
info@toldbyanidiot.org
toldbyanidiot.org

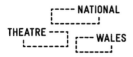

NATIONAL THEATRE WALES
Staff Team

Told by an Idiot

CAST

David Charles
Theatre credits include: *The Dark Philosophers* (National Theatre Wales/Told by an Idiot); *Otieno* (Metta Theatre/Southwark Playhouse); *The Duchess Of Malfi* (Bristol Old Vic); *All Our Hellos and Goodbyes* (LCR/The Gymnasium); *Pedlar* (Lead); *The Invisible Monkey* (New End Theatre) and *An Enemy of the People* (Clwyd Theatre Cymru).

Television credits include: *Fantabulosa* (BBC, in which he played Charles Hawtrey); *M.I.High* (BBC), *High Hopes* (BBC Wales) and *A470* (ITV Wales).

Nia Davies
Theatre credits include: *Six Seeds* (National Theatre); *The Dark Philosophers* (National Theatre Wales/Told by an Idiot); *BBC Children's Prom* (Royal Albert Hall); *Changing Rooms* and *Come Blow Your Horn* (Frinton Summer Theatre); *The Lady Vanishes* (National Tour); and *Merlin and the Cave of Dreams* (Sherman Theatre).

Television credits include: *Y Meees* (S4C).

Nia Gwynne
Theatre credits include: *Look Back In Anger* (Northern Stage Company); *Lie Of The Land* (Edinburgh Festival); *The Daughter In Law*, *Dangerous Corner* and *Love Me Slender* (New Vic); *The Almond and the Seahorse* (Sherman Cymru); *Absurd Person Singular* (Bolton Octagon); *To Kill A Mockingbird* and *The Invention of Love* (Salisbury Playhouse), *Mirandolina* (Royal Exchange), *Ghost City* (Script Cymru/Brits Off Broadway), and *Dogmouth* (The Evidence Room, USA).

Television credits include: *Casualty*, *EastEnders*, *Stick or Twist*, *Belonging* (BBC), *The Bill* (ITV).

Film credits include: *Shadow Dancer* (BBC Films), *Resistance* (Rich Films) and *The Organ Grinder's Monkey*, (Film4/Warp Films).

Ryan Hacker

Theatre credits include: *The Dark Philosophers* (National Theatre Wales/Told by an Idiot); *Carmen* (Leicester Square Theatre); and *Midnight at the Hotel Beuregard* (Rose Bruford College/Paines Plough).

Film credits include: *Hunky Dory* (dir. Marc Evans).

Daniel Hawksford

Theatre credits include: *The Dark Philosophers* (National Theatre Wales/Told by an Idiot); *The Bible – A Recital of The King James Bible*, *Macbeth* and *King Lear* (Globe Theatre); *Dancing at Lughnasa* (Birmingham Rep Theatre); *Judgement Day* (Almeida Theatre); *Much Ado About Nothing* and *The Hour We Knew Nothing of Each Other* (National Theatre); *Troilus and Cressida*, *Romeo and Juliet* and *Rosencrantz And Guildenstern Are Dead* (Clwyd Theatr Cymru); *The School of Night*, *Cymbeline* and *The Taming of the Shrew* (RSC); and *Acqua Nero* (Sgript Cymru).

Television credits include: *Waking the Dead* and *Colditz* (BBC). Film credits include: *Pelican Blood* and *Flesh and Blood*. He is an associate artist for Clwyd Theatr Cymru.

Bettrys Jones

Theatre credits include: *And the Horse You Rode in On* (Told by an Idiot); *The Dark Philosophers* (National Theatre Wales/Told by an Idiot); *The Crucible* (Regents Park Open Air Theatre); *Warhorse* (National Theatre West End); *Measure for Measure* and *Cariad* (Clwyd Theatr Cymru); *Box* (Birmingham Rep); *To Kill a Mockingbird* (West Yorkshire Playhouse); *A Midsummer Night's Dream* (RSC - Novello Theatre); *Comedy Of Errors* (RSC - Novello Theatre/Royal Shakespeare Company); *Quinto Quarto* (Union Theatre, Southwark); *The Little Years* (The Orange Tree Theatre); *Wait Until Dark* (Garrick Theatre/Bill Kenwright Ltd); and *Party Time/One For the Road* (BAC).

Television credits include: *Skins* (E4).

Matthew Owen

Matthew has just graduated from the Royal Welsh College of Music and Drama. This is his first professional role.

Glyn Pritchard

Theatre credits include: *The Dark Philosophers* (National Theatre Wales/Told by an Idiot); *The Black Album* (Tara Arts National Tour); *Othello* (RSC); *The Diver* (Soho Theatre/Tokyo Theatre); *Under Milk Wood* (Tricycle Theatre/London Stage Company); *The Bee* (Noda Map Japan); *A Family Affair* (Arcola Theatre) and *Yn Debyg Iawn i Ti a Fi* (Theatr Genedlaethol Cymru).

Television credits include: *Pobol y Cwm* (BBC Cymru).

Film credits include: *Butterflies* (best short film at Venice Film Festival); *Hunky Dory* (dir. Marc Evans).

Gwyn Thomas (1913-1981)
Gwyn Thomas was born and brought up in Cymmer, in the Rhondda Valley, South Wales. Growing up in poverty, he won a scholarship to Oxford University, and returned to Wales to teach. *The Dark Philosophers* – a collection of short stories – was published in 1946, while his novels include *The Alone to the Alone, All Things Betray Thee, The World Cannot Hear You*, and *Now Lead Us Home*. His play *The Keep* opened at the Royal Court Theatre in 1961, to great acclaim.

Paul Hunter
Director
Paul is co-founder and co-Artistic Director of Told by an Idiot with Hayley Carmichael. He has been involved as director/devisor/performer in all their work to date, including *The Comedy of Errors, The Fahrenheit Twins*, and *Beauty and the Beast*. Other acting credits include: *Troilus and Cressida* and *A Midsummer Night's Dream* (both Shakespeare's Globe), *Rapunzel* (Kneehigh), and *Les Enfants du Paradis* (RSC). He was an Associate Director at the Octagon Theatre, Bolton, where he directed *The Venetian Twins, The Beauty Queen of Leenane* (winner of MEN Award - Best Production), and *Accidental Death of An Anarchist*. His other directing credits include: *Low Pay,*

Don't Pay (Salisbury Playhouse), *Senora Carrar's Rifles* (Young Vic) and the original production of *The Dark Philosophers* (National Theatre Wales/Told by an Idiot) in 2010.

Carl Grose
Writer
Carl has worked previously with Told by an Idiot on *Beauty and the Beast* (Lyric, Hammersmith). His recent plays include: *'Orse Piss for Blood* (The Drum Theatre, Plymouth); *Gargantua* (this year's National Theatre Connections Festival); *Grand Guignol* (The Drum Theatre, Plymouth); *Superstition Mountain* (o-region). He has written for BBC Television and radio, the RSC, Soho Theatre and Vesturport. For the past sixteen years he has worked extensively with Kneehigh Theatre as both actor and writer (writing for Kneehigh includes: *The Wild Bride, Hansel & Gretel, Blast!, Cymbeline* and *Tristan and Yseult*). He also co-founded the Cornish theatre and film production company o-region. Carl first adapted *The Dark Philosophers* for National Theatre Wales/Told By An Idiot for the original production in 2010.

Angela Davies
Designer
Angela designed National Theatre Wales' very first production, *A Good Night Out in the Valleys*. Her previous work includes *Life Is A*

Dream (Donmar Warehouse), and the original production of *The Dark Philosophers* in 2010 (National Theatre Wales/Told by an Idiot). She has designed for companies including the RSC, and for several operas. She has recently designed *Rigoletto* at Grange Park Opera and *The Syndicate* at Chichester/touring.

Ceri James
Lighting Designer
Theatre lighting credits include: *Hansel and Gretel* (Corby Cube); *Salsa* (Theatr na n'Óg); *The Soul Exchange* (National Theatre Wales); *The Butterfly Hunter* (Theatr na n'Óg); *Barkin* (Grass Roots Productions); *Dangerous Liaisons* (Mappa Mundi Theatre); *Broken Hearted* (Derby Theatres); *A Good Night Out in the Valleys* (National Theatre Wales); *Croesi'r Rubicon* (Theatr Bara Caws); *Cinderella* (The Mercury Theatre Colchester); *The BFG* (Fiery Angel/Theatre Royal Northampton); *The Bankrupt Bride* (Theatr na n'Óg); *She Stoops to Conquer* (Mappa Mundi Theatre); *Siwan* (Theatr Genedlaethol Cymru); *Goon Bandage* (Taliesin Arts Centre); *Danny Champion of the World* (Birmingham Stage Company); *The Stories of Hans Christian Anderson* (The Sherman Theatre); *God is a DJ* (Theatre Centre, London); *An Informer's Duty* (The National Youth Theatre of Wales); *Journey to the River Sea* (The Unicorn Theatre); *Martha and the Chinese Elvis* (Salisbury Playhouse); *Beautiful Thing* (Leicester Haymarket Theatre); *The Bat* (New Theatre Stoke on Trent); *Noah* (Oxfordshire Touring Theatre Company).

Iain Johnstone
Composer And Musical Director
As well as a musician, Iain is an actor, director and writer. He is co-artistic director of Wee Stories, Scotland's multi-generational theatre company, with whom he has co-written and directed much of the company's work, including: *Treasure Island*, *One Giant Leap* and the multi-award-winning *Arthur, the Story of a King*. For over 20 years, Iain has worked with most production houses and touring companies in Scottish theatre. With the National Theatre of Scotland, Iain was the tuba-playing Dad in the original production of *Wolves in the Walls*, and most recently played the Emperor in *The Emperor's New Kilt* (winner of the Critics' Award for Theatre in Scotland 2008 for Best Show for Children and Young People), which he also directed and co-wrote.

Gwyn Thomas
By Prof. Dai Smith / Chair – Arts Council of Wales

Gwyn Thomas was born in the Rhondda in 1913. And, as he used to say, 'the next year was even worse'. It was a concentration of Time and Space that conspired to place him at the centre of the maelstrom that was south Wales in the last century. He once hyperbolically claimed that the Rhondda Valleys of his childhood and early manhood were 'a more significant Chicago'. He meant that a great massing of people coming together, largely immigrant and explosive in growth, had turned their mere human aggregation into a congregation of purpose. Out of the most searing poverty and grinding unemployment, which in the 1920s and 1930s had succeeded the dynamic coal capitalism of the 1900s, they had sustained a community through their own intrinsic worth and by expressing its validity in a culture of expressiveness which had scarcely any like on earth. Gwyn became its supreme voice.

From the late 1940s to the early 1950s he published a series of moral fables that took the form of short stories, novellas and full-blown novels but were, in intent, monologues of rhetoric and riffs of dialogue in which savagery was marked by comedy, increasingly black and bilious, and moral judgement was delivered with the stiletto side-step of irony. His protagonists in these European masterpieces were often the collective narrators he called 'we', his Greek chorus laughing hysterically in the wings of history, his Dark Philosophers. These works, of unique style and universal significance, could have been written by no one who had not come from that time and that place.

Success, of a limited kind, brought him wider fame and eventually a loosening of the foothold of security he had found in a mis-fitting career as a school teacher of Spanish. I had encountered him this way as one of his pupils in Barry Grammar School in the 1950s and, thereafter, read him voraciously for his wisdom as much as his incomparable wit. The very fact that he was so funny, in speech and conversation no less than on the page, has sometimes obscured the full force and significance of his meaning, almost as if, for some, on tv and radio, he ended up all wind, and no Chicago. Yet this, in Gwyn's own words in 1952, was to 'look a gift horse in the mouth'. The plain fact is that in a Wales of one-dimensional, one-trick-pony writers, this Genius of Expressiveness had it all and displayed his outrageous facility in plays, newspaper columns, musicals, memoir and fiction, to sing his own song, personal yet collective, notwithstanding the tired conventions of form or genre.

He had even dreamed of a National Theatre of Wales that could embody so much of the things to which he had witnessed during his lifetime. Both *The Keep* in 1962 and *Sap* in 1974, that forerunner of Joan Littlewood's *Oh! What a Lovely War!*, are testimony to his yearning to make drama our own in Wales. He would have been delighted to see National Theatre Wales finally emerge in 2010, and thrilled to know that his Dark Philosophers would, in a new and vital manner, speak their truth and tell their lesson again for this new century. Naturally, they will tell it in such a way as to make their listeners rock with laughter and ache with the pain of their revelatory comedy. How else, Gwyn asked us, would you have it? How else could it be?

Adapted by Carl Grose
and the company

THE DARK PHILOSOPHERS

Based on the life and stories of Gwyn Thomas

OBERON BOOKS
LONDON

WWW.OBERONBOOKS.COM

First published in 2011 by Oberon Books Ltd

521 Caledonian Road, London N7 9RH

Tel: +44 (0) 20 7607 3637 / Fax: +44 (0) 20 7607 3629

e-mail: info@oberonbooks.com

www.oberonbooks.com

A catalogue record for this book is available from the British Library.

ISBN: 978-1-84943-146-0

Cover image by elfen.co.uk

Printed in Great Britain by CPI Antony Rowe, Chippenham.

Characters

GWYN THOMAS

YOUNG GWYN

GWYN'S FATHER – sometimes dead, sometimes not

The People Of The Terraces:

LEWIS – Oscar's whipping boy

NO DOUBT – a loyal employee of Oscar

BEN – a lad so thin he's liable to fall through the cracks in the pavement

THE MACNAFFY ELEMENT – a much-feared resident of Brimstone Terrace

MR & MRS WILSON – landlords of The Harp

HANNAH & DANNY – a couple who have seen better days

NABOTH & ELI – coal miners

COLENSO & EMRYS – Ben's friends

SIMEON – a landowner of dubious repute (keeps goats)

CLARISSE – works behind the bar at The Harp

VERA – a wanna-be singer

BESS, ELSA & ELEANOR – Simeon's daughters

OSCAR – mountain-owner, voter-hater, empire-builder

MEG – his housekeeper

Others:

TV STUDIO RUNNER – Parkinson's whipping boy

MICHAEL PARKINSON – iconic television interviewer

BILLY CONNOLLY & DOLLY PARTON – iconic television celebrities (circa 1970s)

OXFORD STUDENTS – enemies of Gwyn

Simeon's Goats

Oscar's Horse

This text went to press before the end of Rehearsals

The Rhondda Valley, South Wales. Somewhere in the 1930s.

Outside an old pub.

Bird song.

Here is the Welsh author, GWYN THOMAS (in half-mask), sitting next to his younger self, YOUNG GWYN. GWYN's FATHER emerges from the pub, an empty pint glass in his hand.

GWYN'S FATHER: *(Calling into the pub.)* There's nothing wrong with a joke, so long as it's a damned good one! Line me up another!

He throws a dart.

GWYN'S FATHER: I need another drink, son.

YOUNG GWYN: Me too, dad.

GWYN'S FATHER: I shall bring you one. Wait here.

GWYN's FATHER disappears through the pub door. Both GWYNS listen at the door. GWYN's FATHER appears with a bottle of lemonade.

GWYN'S FATHER: Off you go. No listening at the door again.

GWYN THOMAS: I can't think of a healthier place to have your ashes scattered. No noise, no smoke, no traffic. A treat of a view for enduring this joke of a life, don't you think, Gwyn? *Gwyn?*

GWYN'S FATHER: Gwyn?

GWYN THOMAS: Yes, dad?

GWYN'S FATHER: *(To YOUNG GWYN.)* I won't be long. Drink your lemonade. And don't get dark thoughts.

GWYN's FATHER goes back in the pub.

A collection of coal-smudged characters enter for a funeral. It isn't a sombre affair but rather one of pleasant acknowledgement. These people know each other. An urn is passed between them as "All Through The Night" is sung.

SONG: Sleep my child and peace attend thee
   All through the night
   Guardian angels God will send thee
   All through the night
   Soft the drowsy hours are creeping
   Hill and vale in slumber steeping
   I my loving vigil keeping
   All through the night!
   All through the –

The urn's contents are thrown up into the sky. Coal dust is in the air. The characters look ominously upwards. Then run as –

A hundred tons of coal suddenly crashes down from the sky.

GWYN THOMAS brushes the dust off his lapels and takes in the world around him.

Now we're in The Terraces.

GWYN THOMAS: Ah! I know this place.

Enter LEWIS, NO DOUBT, BEN, THE MACNAFFY ELEMENT. They all talk loudly, passionately, with great urgency and desperation (their first lines) – then stop.

GWYN THOMAS: We… in the Terraces tended to live operatically, in shouts. Of the withdrawn or the secluded, there were few. Oh, there was a little of the sly and terrifying madness that simmers on a low flame as in many other places. But on the whole, our freaks were forthright and friendly.

LEWIS: People think I'm a dense crap working for Oscar. Perhaps they're right! But what can I do?

NO DOUBT: I got a nasty crack from a tumbling rock one month previous.

MACNAFFY: Flesh is what I'm after. Hot and heavy and on top of me. I'm only happy when I'm feeling crushed, see?

BEN: Look at me. I'm so thin I'm liable to fall through the cracks in the pavement if I'm not careful!

GWYN THOMAS: With calamity running at a steady rate, silence and withdrawal were taboo. So we made our own music.

BEN: *(Starts to sing beautifully.)*
When I from Havana severed so long a –

(Takes a step forward and disappears through a crack in the pavement.)

Goooooooooooooooooooooooo!!!

GWYN THOMAS: We in the Terraces, terrified of looking inward and becoming too engulfed, frantically watched others. We observed. And we discussed.

MR and MRS WILSON sit at a table.

MR WILSON: You can't judge the whole world by the wretchedness of the Terraces, Mrs Wilson.

MRS WILSON: That's your bloody father talking that is, Mr Wilson!

MR WILSON: You been living on a diet of politics and dry toast for too long!

MRS WILSON: Definitely your father! It's either that or your glands.

MR WILSON: Don't you blame my father, Mrs Wilson! And don't you blame my glands!

They argue furiously, in silence.

GWYN THOMAS: We spent our time philosophising over the behaviour of our fellow man. It kept our minds off things. Oh, we liked our philosophy the way we liked our tea. Dark.

HANNAH: It's a blessed relief, this job you've found, Danny. Now mind your back and bring home coal.

GWYN THOMAS: Hannah! *(Clutches his heart.)* Hannah was strong-looking. With the most beautiful face that had ever been seen in all the valley.

HANNAH sings the 1930's song, "Body and Soul".

SONG: I'm lost in the dark
    Where is the spark for my love?

GWYN THOMAS: Oh yes, the front doors of the Terraces stood open. It served to reduce the smell of damp rot in these murky dwellings. It allowed for folk to flow to and from the houses. It allowed for gentle song to drift and mingle…

SONG: The heavens opened and closed
    As well I might have supposed
    And I am lost in dis-abandon
    So far removed from all that I had planned on…

GWYN THOMAS: And when inevitably we folk got to argue, punches were thrown.

A brawl breaks out. It tumbles and spreads out into the Terraces as the song gets sweeter and fuller.

SONG: My days have grown so lonely
    For I have lost my one and lonely
    My pride has been humbled
    But I am his body and soul

    I was a mere sensation
    My house of cards had no foundation
    Although it has tumbled
    I still am his body and soul
    I still am his body and soul

An explosion from the mine shakes up the house and, indeed, the whole Terrace.

Underground.

Miners work in the darkness about them. NABOTH KINSEY and ELI scrape away in a hole. ELI stops work whenever he can.

ELI: You know, Naboth, you're like me you are. You've got a feeling for where the seams run. For us it's simple. The coal is somewhere underneath, so down we go, straight as a plummet. That's a fine deep hole you've got here, Naboth.

It's straight. And it's deep. When do you think you'll hit the main seam, Nab?

NABOTH: There's no hurry, Eli. We'll take it nice and steady.

ELI: I know you, Naboth. You're not given to long idle arguments about method like me, a noted theorist. I know you scorn those level workings. Me too! To hell with levels! Let's go down as perpendicularly as we can!

He scrapes and scrapes.

ELI: Out of interest, Nab… just how far are you planning on digging? Cus it'll take a long old time, this.

NABOTH: I do not feel rushed, Eli.

ELI: That's the spirit! That's what I like to hear! A man who enjoys his work!

He scrapes.

ELI: Boy, this hole is deep!

Explosion!

Street.

Two lads, COLENSO & EMRYS, play football with a lump of coal. A third boy, BEN, sits and sings a song.

SONG: When I from Havana severed so long ago
No one knew but thee what joy I left behind

They freeze. GWYN appears and scores a goal.

GWYN THOMAS: He shoots, he scores! *(To us.)* Well, have you tried playing rugby with a lump of coal?

The action resumes, and the song brings forth an old man with a walking stick. This is SIMEON.

SONG: And yet there are many dearer to thee
I know
So still to its fate my heart must be resigned
If at thy pain a beautiful dove comes winging
Treat it with kindness, for my own thoughts…

They all stare at SIMEON.

SIMEON: Any of you boys out of work?

COLENSO: I'm fine. I go up and down ladders. Father wants me to be a roofer, like him.

SIMEON: You?

EMRYS: I've just gone into the pit as butty to my uncle who's a mean sort of sod.

SIMEON: What about you?

BEN: No one'll give me a job, Mr Simeon.

SIMEON: Oh?

EMRYS: Look at him. He's so thin he's liable to fall through the cracks in the pavement.

SIMEON: Well, you seem to be the worst off of the lot!

BEN: I'm pretty bad off, Mr Simeon.

SIMEON: How'd you like a job with me?

GWYN THOMAS: *(In BEN's ear.)* Say "Yes please, Mr Simeon."

BEN: Yes please, Mr Simeon.

SIMEON: You know my farm? On the mountain? Way up there?

BEN nods.

SIMEON: Come by first thing Monday and I'll put you to work.

BEN: Thank you, Mr. Simeon.

SIMEON goes.

COLENSO: Simeon's not right, you know.

BEN: You're just jealous.

COLÈNSO: Preacher says the goats he keeps got something to do with it.

BEN: Goats? There's nothing wrong with goats, is there, Emrys?

EMRYS: There's nothing wrong with anybody.

COLENSO: It depends on what you do with them, though, isn't it? He's a bad man.

BEN: I've got to work, Colenso.

COLENSO: We all do. But there's a limit, surely, to the lengths you'd go?

Explosion!

Mine.

NABOTH scrapes in the darkness.

Explosion!

Street.

Enter CLARISSE and VERA from one side and LEWIS, a young lad of 19, from the other. He walks by them.

CLARISSE: 'lo Lewis.

LEWIS: 'lo Clarisse.

VERA: Lewis.

LEWIS: Vera.

GWYN THOMAS: Lewis had, at some time or other, chased most of the girls in the Terraces, but had grown tired of it. Now the girls chased him.

CLARISSE: You could boil a bloody egg to those blasts, eh?

LEWIS: Eh?

VERA: Every three minutes, aren't they?

LEWIS: Oh. I see. Yeh, I suppose you could. Boil. An egg.

CLARISSE: See you at the Harp tonight?

LEWIS: If Oscar's thirsty, I'll be there.

CLARISSE watches LEWIS exit.

CLARISSE: Dark.

VERA: You will come to the Coliseum this evening won't you, Clarisse? To watch me sing, like you said?

CLARISSE: Not tonight, Vera. I've got to work.

VERA: Clarisse? Clarisse, you promised!

CLARISSE goes. VERA follows.

Explosion!

NABOTH scrapes. He hears Verdi drifting in from somewhere and is drawn to it. He walks into –

The Coliseum Cinema.

GWYN THOMAS: Now this is my favourite part. It's where I get to play the theatre manager. Not many lines, but it's a peach of a part.

An excited rabble enters. GWYN checks their tickets. They take their seats.

GWYN THOMAS: *(Backstage.)* You're up next, Vera.

VERA squirts her mouth.

GWYN THOMAS: And now ladies and gentlemen, the next act of the evening is…

A BOY scampers in, late. The crowd tut and groan.

GWYN THOMAS: Ladies and gentlemen, please put your hands together for… Miss Vera Fisher!

The crowd – cheers then waits expectantly. It slowly dawns on them that VERA's singing is utterly dreadful.

GWYN THOMAS: Unfortunately, Vera's voice did not sound as good in public as it did in her own bedroom.

The crowd flees in horror.

Outside The Harp.

LEWIS stands in a narrow column of constant pelting rain. GWYN THOMAS, watching him, remains magically dry. Enter CLARISSE from pub. She has black hair and a red blouse. When the door opens, the singing intensifies.

CLARISSE: Come on in here, Lewis.

LEWIS: Nah thanks, Clarisse.

CLARISSE: Don't be daft. You'll catch your death!

LEWIS doesn't move.

CLARISSE: Come on. I've got tea made.

LEWIS looks at CLARISSE standing framed in the doorway. He takes a step toward her. Suddenly, LEWIS's DEAD DAD sits up out of his grave in a shower of coal dust.

DEAD DAD: Watch yourself there, boy!

LEWIS: Not now, dad.

DEAD DAD: You're a good-for-nothing bloody nuisance! Eyes all over that scarlet blouse!

LEWIS: I've heard it all before.

DEAD DAD: And still you don't listen!

LEWIS: You're dead. Keep your thoughts to yourself.

DEAD DAD: I may be dead but I'm still your dad.

LEWIS: An element does not have to be like his old man.

DEAD DAD: Just drink in the smooth redness of the blouse from a safe distance is all I advise!

LEWIS goes to CLARISSE.

DEAD DAD: Mark my words. It'll all go to hell if you accept that cup of tea!

DEAD DAD sinks down into the earth.

CLARISSE: Well, are you coming or not?

LEWIS doesn't budge.

CLARISSE: We can go in back where there's some quiet.

LEWIS: I'm waiting for Oscar. I've got to take him home.

CLARISSE: Oscar's well away. He's got that Macnaffy element from Brimstone Terrace hanging off him. He'll be a while yet.

LEWIS: Best I wait for him here.

They stare at each other. CLARISSE puts her hands over her head and runs into the rain towards him. They kiss.

CLARISSE: You're big and dark and strong.

LEWIS: Tell me something I don't know.

CLARISSE: Dark and strong, Lewis, like the man in the book I'm reading.

LEWIS: I didn't know you could read.

She whaps him.

CLARISSE: Why don't you ever go with girls, Lew?

LEWIS: I haven't got the time. Or the fancy.

CLARISSE: That Oscar in there, he's a hog.

LEWIS: He is that, twice over.

CLARISSE: Then why'd you work for him? There's folk round here say you're a dense crap for doing so.

LEWIS: Perhaps they're right. Tell him to hurry up with that Macnaffy element will you? I'll be too stiff to take him home if he keeps me waiting in the dark much longer.

CLARISSE: It'll be dark on that mountain, Lewis. Darker than you.

LEWIS: Oscar does it blind on a regular basis. The dark doesn't matter much.

CLARISSE: Why don't you get a decent job, Lewis?

LEWIS: I got one, Clarisse. This is it.

CLARISSE: I mean a good, useful job where you could get married.

LEWIS: Because Oscar gave me a job when no one else would, and as for being married – I keep my mother.

CLARISSE: Oh well. I'll tell Oscar to put a move on then.

She kisses him again and goes back in.

GWYN chats to the goats as they build –

SIMEON's farm.

GWYN THOMAS: Now that's something you don't see every day. Two goats moving a table. Very clever animals goats. This one does my accounts.

SIMEON is eating as BEN enters.

BEN: I'm here, Mr. Simeon.

SIMEON: God. I'd forgotten how thin you were! I wonder if I haven't made a terrible mistake by having you here.

BEN: You haven't, Mr. Simeon. You'll see.

SIMEON hands BEN a bowl of food. BEN devours it.

Two GOATS bleat attracting BEN's attention.

SIMEON: First things first, there's the outhouses need cleaning. After that you can hoe the vegetable plots. Are you listening?

BEN: Goats.

One GOAT chews the leg of BEN's trousers.

SIMEON: Goats? Yes, goats. I have goats. I'll have you working late and starting early, so you can take a bed here if you're tired.

BEN: If that's all right, Mr Simeon?

SIMEON: I've said it is. You can have my youngest daughter's room.

BEN: Oh, Mr. Simeon I –

SIMEON: Don't panic. She's not here.

BEN: Thanks, Mr. Simeon. This is much better than having my
    life constantly threatened by those cracks in the pavement.

SIMEON: It's nice to have the company. Now hoe.

BEN sings "La Paloma" as he works. The GOATS join in.

SONG: Ah, my darling so dear, bid it no more to roam
    But say thou'lt follow it dearest one ever
    Into my mountain home

*A GOAT mops his brow. He catches his breath, then continues hoeing
and singing.*

Ah, my darling so dear!
Bid it no more to roam
But say thou wilt follow it dearest
Even to my mountain home
O, come to me, O, come to me
My heart is longing for thee love for thee!

Dusk falls.

The kitchen.

*SIMEON sits at the table, a glass of beer in his hand, listening to
the boy.*

SONG: Fly with my little dove o'er land and sea
    Fly with it darling to me, yes, to me…

SIMEON: God Ben, it's a hell of a thing sometimes, this *living*.

Night.

*BEN, with candle, edges down a corridor in SIMEON's house.
Suddenly, a door opens a crack right before him – two pale wide-
eyed girls stare at him.*

FIRST GIRL: Who are you?

SECOND GIRL: What are you doing here?

FIRST GIRL: Run away!

SECOND GIRL: Run away!

The door slams shut.

SIMEON: *(From downstairs.)* Found your room all right, boy?

BEN: *(Unnerved.)* Yes. Got it. Good night.

GWYN blows his candle out.

Back to The Harp.

LEWIS standing in the rain.

Enter MRS WILSON from the pub.

MRS WILSON: Lewis? You'll have to come and get Oscar. He's heard a hymn and fallen face down in a puddle of his own sweat.

LEWIS: Right-o, Mrs Wilson.

GWYN THOMAS: Seeing Mrs Wilson there in the doorway after looking at Clarisse was like looking at a grate from which the fire had been scraped out.

MRS WILSON: He's in his little room down on the left.

LEWIS: I know the room, Mrs Wilson.

SIMEON's house.

BEN, in bed, reads a cowboy book. The pages light up his face, and the muffled sound of galloping horses and gunfire fill the room.

From outside, voices. BEN closes the book and listens.

GIRL'S VOICE: What are you doing?

SIMEON Goddammit, I'm your father aren't I?

GIRL'S VOICE: *(Screaming.)* See yourself there you pig! See yourself there you pig! See yourself there you pig!

BEN blocks out the screaming by opening the book and delving into the world of the Wild West again – Smith and Wesson gunfire just about manages to block out the screaming outside his room.

SIMEON suddenly puts his head round the door, enters, sits on the edge of the bed.

SIMEON: Anyone ever hate you, Ben, like they hate me? See that nobody does. It's a hell of a messy feeling it gives you.

SIMEON leans in and tickles BEN on the chest. BEN giggles.

SIMEON: Do you like goats, Ben?

BEN: Goats? They're all right.

SIMEON: Could you love a goat?

BEN: What would you want to love a goat for?

SIMEON: What would you want to love anything for?

BEN: I don't know, Mr. Simeon. I'm pretty young.

SIMEON: If goats could talk and answer to your love, a man wouldn't have to worry about his soul.

From outside, BEN hears the goat bleat.

Next morning. Kitchen.

BEN sits at the table.

Enter a pale, miserable-looking woman from upstairs. This is BESS. She and BEN stare at each other.

BESS: Where is he?

BEN: Who?

BESS: My father.

BEN: Out.

BESS: Where's he gone?

BEN: For a walk.

BESS: *(Calling up.)* Come down, Elsa. He's out for a spell.

Enter ELSA, younger than BESS but with a similar complexion.

ELSA: *(Off, to her child.)* Stay there.

BESS: It's nice to see this part of the house again for a change.

ELSA: It's nice and cool.

BEN: *(Looking, off.)* Is that your boy?

BESS: What did he bring you here for?

BEN: To help him work.

ELSA: He needs no help.

BESS: The best thing you can do, boy, is go away from here.

ELSE & BESS: We told you that.

BEN I'd rather not. There's nothing for me down in the Terraces.

BESS exits to the garden outside.

BEN: What's the matter with her?

ELSA: She doesn't like my father.

BEN: Why?

ELSA: You're thin.

BEN: Never eat much.

She gives BEN a kiss.

ELSA: What girls do you know and what do you do to them?

BEN: I don't know any girls.

She stares at BEN for a moment, then bursts into laughter and shoves him in disbelief.

ELSA: How old are you?

BEN: Sixteen last.

ELSA: Same age as Eleanor.

BEN: Who's Eleanor?

ELSA: My sister.

BEN: Where's she?

ELSA: She's not here.

BEN: How's that?

ELSA: Bess sent her away.

BEN: Why?

ELSA: Bess wanted Eleanor out of the old man's way.

BEN: Oh.

ELSA: Has he done anything to you yet?

BEN: Like what?

ELSA: Anything unusual?

BEN: No.

ELSA looks to her child, off.

ELSA: This is – what's your name?

BEN: Ben.

ELSA: Ben. Say "hullo" to Ben. Shy.

BEN: Kids are, as a rule.

ELSA: Who's he like? Does he look like me?

BEN: No.

ELSA: Who's he like then, if he isn't like me?

BEN looks at the BOY.

BEN: Simeon. He's the spitting image of Simeon.

ELSA suddenly cries at this.

GWYN THOMAS: *(Into BEN's ear.)* Say "There, there. No need to cry."

BEN: There, there. No need to cry.

ELSA: Isn't there?

BEN: Where's Bess?

ELSA: Tending to the cabbages.

BESS is at the bottom of the cabbage patch, on her knees. She sobs.

BEN: *(Looking out.)* Why's she weeping over them?

GWYN THOMAS: Say "It's been a tricky summer…"

ELSA: It's been a tricky summer.

BEN: They don't look the crop they might've been but... even so... crying over a cabbage?

Enter SIMEON swinging his walking stick.

SIMEON: *(Seeing the BOY.)* Who brought *that* down?

Get him out of my bloody sight! I told you to keep him out of my way! I go sick at the sight of him! You understand that? Sick! Where's that Bess?

BEN looks to the window. SIMEON looks out to the garden, then flies out of the kitchen taking his stick with him. BEN watches from the window.

ELSA: What's he doing?

BESS is beaten by SIMEON.

SIMEON: *(Yelling.)* Get up! Get up now!

BESS lifts herself up, and is struck again.

SIMEON: I told you, didn't I? Told you not to come down here! Get inside! Go on!

ELSA, terrified, runs upstairs with the BOY.

Enter SIMEON pushing BESS into the kitchen. She trembles with pain.

SIMEON: If I catch you down in that garden again it'll be worse than the stick you'll get.

BESS: You can't hurt me anymore.

SIMEON Don't be too sure of that.

BESS: You're a bloody devil.

SIMEON: That's part of it.

BESS: You've made a pretty mess of us all with your bloody lust.

SIMEON: A man's got to love somebody.

BESS: Only a devil could stand there and grin about it. But there's one thing I'm thankful for even in this hell on earth you've given us here. My baby and Elsa's are boys. Which means you'll never want them, will you? You'll never go mad after their bodies and hearts. You'll never destroy the things they love. They'll be men when they grow up and you'll be old and weak. And sometimes I hope they'll be as mad as you are, mad and cruel, so you'll be as afraid of them like we're afraid of you. You wanted Eleanor too… but you didn't have her. She's safe. I sent her away. I saw to it, didn't I? Bit cleverer than you were there eh, wasn't I?

GWYN THOMAS: *(To SIMEON.)* Start laughing.

SIMEON laughs.

BESS: What are you laughing at?

GWYN THOMAS: Laugh more.

SIMEON: *(Laughing.)* I'm laughing at you.

BESS: Why are you laughing at me?

SIMEON: Because Eleanor is coming back.

BESS: Coming back?

SIMEON: Her aunt is dead so they're sending Eleanor back to me, back to her home with me, where she belongs. And let me warn you. When Eleanor comes, I don't want you or Elsa to speak a word to her. Not a word, understand? If you do, you'll be sorry.

BESS slowly exits upstairs.

SIMEON drinks. Throughout the following, GWYN keeps SIMEON's glass topped up.

SIMEON: Life's got sharp eyes boy, and a nasty heart. If you're weak, whang, you get its foot right in your neck. Do you want life's foot in your neck, Benny?

BEN: No fear.

SIMEON: Then drink, boy. Let's drink to Venus!

SIMEON drinks.

SIMEON: Sing.

BEN: What song would you like?

SIMEON: The doves, Benny. I don't want to hear anything but the doves.

BEN: I'm wearing the wings off those doves, seems to me.

SIMEON: Sing, Benny.

SIMEON drinks. Lots.

BEN: *(Sings.)* If at thy pain a beautiful dove comes winging
Treat it with kindness, for my own thoughts tis bring –

SIMEON: Whatever men have said about beauty, you could have said about her.

BEN: Who?

SIMEON: My wife, Benny. Christ, her kindness.

BEN: Where is she?

GWYN THOMAS: *(In SIMEON's ear.)* Say "She died."

SIMEON: She died. That was the end of it, boy. She died.

BEN: People do.

SIMEON: What you say?

BEN: People do die. Very common around where I live.

SIMEON drinks.

SIMEON: When she died, I said I'd keep on loving her. I said I'd love all the things she'd ever seen… touched… made. Dresses, curtains…

GWYN THOMAS: Even the kids.

SIMEON Even the kids. God, yes. Even the kids. She made them, didn't she? But that was a cruel thing for me to do,

Benny. A hell of a rotten, cruel thing to do, and sometimes when I think of it I could…

(He drinks.)

I said I'd love that woman til I died, love her with my body like I'd always loved her. And I'll never change til I die…

(His head drops drowsily.)

No, I'll never change…

GWYN THOMAS: Now go to sleep.

SIMEON is asleep.

BEN, with GWYN's help, lays SIMEON out on the table.

The box-room.

A candle burns. BEN in bed. Western opened but unread.

Enter BESS.

BESS: You've got to help us, Benny.

BEN: Me? What can I do?

BESS: Don't act so stupid. You've got to!

BEN: But look at me. I'm underweight. I'm so thin I'm liable to fall through the cracks in the pavement if I'm not careful. Everybody says that.

BESS: Help us or I'll pull your ears off!

BEN: All right.

BESS: He wants to ruin her like he ruined us.

BEN: Ruin who?

BESS: Eleanor. She's young, like you. Make her your friend. Be with her at all times. Keep her away from my father as if he was the plague. Tell her to get away from this house, understand me? Make her listen to you. Tell her to get away!

BEN: Make Eleanor my friend. Right.

A GOAT bleats.

BESS: But be careful. My father doesn't like boys who try to take his daughters away from him. He's mad, you see? If he finds you trying to take Eleanor away – which is what you have to do! – he'll want to kill you.

BEN: Killing's a bit much though, isn't it?

BESS: There was once a man who wanted to take me away. He's was a fine lad. Thin, like you, but tall and strong. He would've done anything for me. He died because my father wanted him to die. His name was Walter James Mathias.

BEN: I've heard of him. Folk said he was the biggest ram around. He just upped and left.

BESS: He's dead now.

BEN: You're telling me Simeon killed –

BESS: I didn't say anything.

BEN: But shouldn't the police –

BESS: What happened to Walter James Mathias is my business, my father's and Walter's. And where he sleeps, he's near to me. Very near to me, and that's good.

When Eleanor comes, don't let her out of your sight.

She leaves the room.

Back to The Harp.

MRS WILSON: *(GWYN's ventriloquist dummy.)* Lewis? You'll have to come and get Oscar. He's heard a hymn and fallen face down in a puddle of his own sweat.

MACNAFFY, a thin, young, savage-faced girl, flees from the pub and collides with LEWIS.

MACNAFFY: He's a bloody weight that Oscar is!

LEWIS: Been playing him like a piano, have you?

MACNAFFY: He did let out a brief snort of a tune.

GWYN THOMAS: Her face was tired, thin and savage. You could imagine her coming from a place called Brimstone Terrace. She was the sort of element who had been steadily preached against ever since preaching started.

MACNAFFY: What do you feed him on?

LEWIS: Acorns. And twice a year I bathe him in swill.

MACNAFFY: What gives Oscar the right to think he can go around expecting girls to lie at his feet like mats to be jumped on?

LEWIS: Did he jump on you?

MACNAFFY: Got me drunk. Got me in there. Next thing I know, the whole bloody roof's come down!

The rumble and hiss of an approaching train - a whistle blows, a blast of steam. It clears to reveal ELEANOR, standing on the platform, suitcase in hand. BEN, beside her, smiles.

SIMEON's kitchen.

SIMEON, BEN and ELEANOR sit around the table. They pick at their food but are clearly more interested in each other. SIMEON does not eat. He watches ELEANOR.

SIMEON: Make this house your little world, Eleanor. Stay close to home now. You're so much like your mother, Eleanor. It's as if she's come back. Your eyes, her hair… Don't try to be too friendly with your sisters. They're very jealous of you. You'll soon see that. But I can't blame them for not liking you. You are so very beautiful.

GWYN THOMAS: Now touch her face.

SIMEON touches ELEANOR's face.

SIMEON: They're jealous, your sisters, and best not spoken to. Whatever you want to say, say it to your father. He'll always want to listen. Of course, there's Benny here. But don't pay him too much attention. He's so thin he's liable to fall through the cracks in the pavement. It makes you laugh sometimes to watch him eat.

SIMEON laughs. BEN forces a smile but his hands are tightly clenched fists.

Later.

The wood block.

SIMEON chops wood.

BEN hoes the vegetable plot... he stops at the cabbage patch. He bends to inspect them... BEN's attention goes to SIMEON. The man swings the axe down with terrific force. BEN imagines himself at the mercy of SIMEON's strength. SIMEON stops and glares at BEN. As do the GOATS.

Kitchen.

ELEANOR passes a cup of tea to BEN. Their fingers touch. SIMEON sees this. Swings his axe –

Explosion!

The kitchen. Night.

SIMEON stares at BEN who sits at the table. He cuts some bread with the knife and eats.

SIMEON: You like my daughter, Benny?

BEN: Yes.

SIMEON: She's nice.

BEN: She's grand.

GWYN grabs BEN and throws him onto the table, his hands at BEN's neck.

SIMEON: You lean, miserable little bastard! There are laws for those who take my daughters! They are my laws, just as they are my daughters. Mine! Do you hear that? Every tiny, mortal, bloody scrap of them, mine. You must be made to stop loving, Benny. You must be made to stop, like that other lean and hungry ram was made to stop. And I'm the one to stop you. He died easy, that other. And so will you, Benny boy!

GWYN brings his knee up into SIMEON's groin.

Enter ELEANOR.

SIMEON: Eleanor…

SIMEON staggers towards her.

Enter BESS and ELSA from upstairs.

BESS: Leave her alone!

BESS has the bread knife. GWYN takes it and drives it into SIMEON. SIMEON collapses back onto the table, and emits a choked scream. ELSA runs to his side.

BEN runs to ELEANOR.

BESS: It's alright, Eleanor. He's dead. He's dead and I did it. He's dead and I did it.

ELSA stares blankly at SIMEON's corpse.

BESS, at the cabbage patch, starts to sing.

SONG: O come to me, O come to me
My heart is longing for thee, for thee
My soul is sighing where'er I be
My heart is longing for thee, for thee
Fly with my little dove o'er land and sea
Fly with it darling to me, to me…

BEN takes ELEANOR's hand and exits.

We are left with this tragic scene for a moment, then –

A RUNNER from a British 1970s chat show appears.

RUNNER: Five minutes, Mr Parkinson.

SIMEON's corpse sits up and becomes MICHAEL PARKINSON. Chairs are wheeled in, a flurry of last minute studio activity, the lights come up and –

RUNNER: We are ready to go in – five four three…

The "Parkinson" theme starts.

PARKY: Thank you, ladies and gentlemen, and welcome. My first guest is one of Scotland's finest comedians. Please put your hands together for – Billy Connolly.

Enter BILLY CONNOLLY.

PARKY: Great to see you again, Billy. I seem to remember the last time you were here you almost had me taken off the air.

BILLY: Aye, that's right, Michael.

PARKY: Where does this humour of yours come from?

BILLY: I get a lot of it from Glasgow, where I'm from. For instance, this guy Gregor, I met him in the pub one night. I said, Gregor, how's the wife? He said, Billy, she's dead. I said, What dead?

BILLY fast forwards.

BILLY: - and there's this bottom sticking out the ground, and he says, "I've got to park mah bike somewhere!"

Laughter and applause.

PARKY: Thank you very much, Billy Connolly!

Applause.

PARKY: Now, my second guest comes all the way from Memphis, Tennessee. Performing her latest song her tonight, please welcome – Miss Dolly Parton.

Enter DOLLY PARTON, who starts to sing. Fast forward. SONG ends. Applause. DOLLY joins PARKINSON and BILLY.

DOLLY: Howdy, boys.

BILLY: Hello, Dolly.

PARKY: Now my final guest tonight (and the one you've all been waiting for) is a very Welsh Welshman. Born in the Rhondda valley, the son of a miner, he became a teacher, novelist, playwright and television personality in that order.

To date, he's written 14 books, 3 plays and is probably best remembered in television for his work in the Brain's Trust, where he distinguishes himself as a marvellous talker – ladies and gentlemen, Gwyn Thomas.

Wild applause.

GWYN THOMAS enters from somewhere bizarre, and sits.

(The following section is improvised for each performance, but here is an approximation of what might be said.)

PARKY: I was going to ask you, Gwyn, why you chose to live in Wales. In fact, you're still living in the same area you were born in. Why is that? Is it that the writer needs to be near his home?

GWYN THOMAS: I think it's got a lot to do with my mother. I'm the youngest of twelve children, which is quite a load to bear humanly speaking. I don't know how it is in other parts of the world, but in Wales, if you were the youngest of a very large family, you were the chopping block for the lot. All the frustrations – frustrations in politics, love, ambition – they all take it out on the youngest. And my mother died when I was very young, and I think I had this feeling that there… there was some primeval security, security of the womb that I had rather missed, you see? And I have tended to stay near this valley where I was born. Which is another way of saying that as soon as I get to Chepstow I feel very frightened and turn back!

PARKY: You once said that every Welshman is a kind of mobile theatre – what exactly did you mean by that?

GWYN THOMAS: I mean, they have ways of telling the time that make you think they've invented the clock! "It's ten to nine! It's ten to nine! I'm a liar! It's FIVE to nine, you see!" And in the Rhondda Valley, this is a very strange thing… I looked like thousands of other people. You know, dark and short and broad.

And I must have looked like so many people that time and again people have come up to me in the street, and tugged,

"Bron's pregnant!" I didn't know who Bron was. No idea! "Councillor Dors is at it again!" Of course, this is very good for a writer to…

PARKY: Exploit?

GWYN THOMAS: Exactly! Oh, it was a very dramatic society, there's no doubt about that…

Music begins to drift in from the Terraces.

GWYN THOMAS: There's no doubt about that at all…

GWYN stands.

BILLY: You alright, Gwyn?

DOLLY: Mr. Thomas? Are you OK?

GWYN steps back into the Terraces. The TV studio vanishes.

Here, the Terraces are strangely becalmed. GWYN THOMAS wanders the streets, looking through windows, looking in at the lives of those in the Terraces.

They all sing.

SONG: There's a hope that leaves me never
     All through the night…
     All through the night…

Outside The Harp.

Still raining.

GWYN THOMAS: The place was plagued by floods. Rain was intense and the valley narrow. Young Edwin said the roof in his house leaked so much he had floated from one bedroom to another and had to be rowed back by his father.

Rain drops onto GWYN's newspaper. The water level rises. GWYN tries to bail out the water with his hat. He drowns. And gets rescued by someone in a kayak.

MACNAFFY collides with LEWIS.

MACNAFFY: He's a bloody weight that Oscar is!

LEWIS: Been playing him like a piano, have you?

MACNAFFY: He did let out a brief snort of a tune. What do you feed him on?

LEWIS: Acorns. And twice a year I bathe him in swill.

MACNAFFY: What gives Oscar the right to think he can go around expecting girls to lie at his feet like mats to be jumped on?

LEWIS: Did he jump on you?

MACNAFFY: Got me drunk. Got me in there. Next thing I know, the whole bloody roof's come down!

LEWIS: It's cus he owns a mountain.

MACNAFFY: Oh? And what sort of god does that make him?

LEWIS: If you own a mountain you can pretty much jump on what you like. There's a big coal-tip on top of the mountain and Oscar owns that too. Plus thirty odd people who work on the tip picking coal and putting it in sacks for him to sell. He's got money as well as mountains, see? As far as Oscar goes, there's nobody bigger than Oscar.

MACNAFFY: How old are you?

LEWIS: Past nineteen.

MACNAFFY: You seem to know a lot about life.

LEWIS: I know a lot about Oscar.

MACNAFFY: What a bloody weight.

LEWIS: What a bloody life.

MACNAFFY: What's your name, boy?

LEWIS: Lewis.

MACNAFFY: So long Lewis.

MACNAFFY dons her hat and pushes her face into the wall and rubs it back and forth viciously (a bizarre and disturbing sight.)

MACNAFFY: And best of luck getting that big fat bastard back up his mountain!

MR WILSON, the landlord, appears.

MR WILSON: Please! I have owned this establishment for years and I have never heard such profanity!

MACNAFFY: Oh, up your ass you prudish old tit!

EXIT MACNAFFY, banging the door behind her.

LEWIS: Give us a hand would you, Mr Wilson?

MR WILSON: Absolutely. I'd like him out of my pub. It's very late you know.

LEWIS: Yes. I know.

MR WILSON: He's all right as long as he keeps singing.

LEWIS: Then keep him singing.

MR WILSON: He loses interest around ten, when the hymns start. Is Oscar a pagan, Lewis?

LEWIS: God knows what he is, Mr. Wilson.

OSCAR, a huge, rattling, groaning thing made of jacket and wig, bursts through the door.

OSCAR turns and pukes. He collapses to the floor and crawls. LEWIS hauls him to his feet.

LEWIS leads OSCAR up the mountain.

The congregation sing.

SONG: Excavator! Oscar!
Voter-hater! Oscar!
Empire-builder (builder)
With his hand
Mountain-claimer (claimer)
Shapes the land…

The horse and OSCAR appear smaller now, as they curve up the mountain.

SONG Hallelujah!
Hallelujah!
Hallelujah,
Hallelujah
We will praise him for his love
Praise the father (father)
Sat above!

Explosion!

GWYN's FATHER bursts through a door.

GWYN'S FATHER: Here! My Gwyn is off to Oxford University! Oxford University, no less!

The YOUNG GWYN, looking tiny in a huge and heavy coat, walks down the streets, loaded with bags. Neighbours wave to him from their doorsteps.

TERRACER: Who made your overcoat, Gwyn?

YOUNG GWYN: Mr. Warlow.

TERRACER: I hear his best customers have been gnomes!

GWYN'S FATHER: Pay no attention, Gwyn. That overcoat will impress the English. Make them less bossy.

YOUNG GWYN, breaking under the weight of it, forges on.

GWYN THOMAS: On the morning of my departure for the ancient university I shuffled down the hill to the coach station feeling like an emperor and looking like a cross between Humphry Bogart and a shrouded dwarf.

GWYN'S FATHER: Come on, Gwyn, you're almost there!

YOUNG GWYN: It's this coat, da. It's heavy as lead. I'm exhausted.

GWYN'S FATHER: All right you lot. Help the boy on his last ten yards, will you?

The people of the Terraces pick YOUNG GWYN up and carry him to the coach.

THE TERRACES: Good bye, Gwyn!

They wave him off.

GWYN THOMAS: To me, absurdity is the most beautiful thing.

Explosion!

OSCAR's house. A dark kitchen.

Enter MEG from pantry.

MEG: Where's Oscar?

LEWIS: He's in his room, Meg. I've never seen him look so daft.

MEG: Must be his brain starting to dissolve as a result of all the stuff he drinks.

She goes through a door to where OSCAR is.

MEG: *(Off.)* Here. Drink some tea. Then eat something. Come on. You're always hungry. You eat like a goat most times.

From within, OSCAR groans.

MEG: What's the matter with him?

LEWIS: He's tired.

MEG: Who's he been with?

LEWIS: Some element from Brimstone Terrace.

MEG: Oh.

LEWIS: She looked like a bag. Didn't like Oscar much. He crushed her flat.

MEG sighs, then removes her shirt. LEWIS lights a cigarette, and watches her go back in to OSCAR.

OSCAR: *(Within.)* Get out of my sight!

MEG comes out, buttoning herself up.

MEG: Not even the sight of flesh can coax his snoring desires from their rat-holes this night.

LEWIS: Get your clothes on, Meg. Nothing will stir him much before Christmas.

He hands her his cigarette.

MEG: You know, Lew, you can kill a cat or a dog and nobody bats an eye. But if you did away with this beast there'd be a hell of a howl.

LEWIS: Don't try it, Meg. He's not worth the trouble.

MEG: Maybe he is. Maybe he isn't.

LEWIS: Good night, Meg.

MEG: Good night, Lew.

Mountain.

LEWIS walks home. A wind blows. Shutters and doors rattle. The landscape seems to "breathe" OSCAR.

OSCAR: *(Disembodied voice.)* Get out of my bloody sight!

LEWIS: Oscar? Somebody there?

A door creaks open, a hand emerges…

LEWIS: Oscar?

No. It's DEAD DAD.

LEWIS: Ah, Christ, da'!

DEAD DAD: You're seeing Oscar bloody everywhere, you are!

LEWIS: I am. I see his black beady eyes in the coal. His fat round face in the moon. His huge shape in the mountain. Christ, he is, he's bloody everywhere! Everywhere I look - down, up, sideways, inside, out - there's Oscar!

DEAD DAD: It's late, boy. Take some rest.

The Terraces.

GWYN THOMAS: Each house in the Terrace was one of a hundred in a row and just like the other ninety-nine, you see? Even the smell was the same in every home that of cabbage, of damp, and rent.

LEWIS: *(Entering his house, calling.)* I'm home!

DEAD DAD appears from nowhere.

DEAD DAD: Shh! Your mother's asleep.

LEWIS: Good. I get uncomfortable with her sitting there with that far-away look in her eyes.

DEAD DAD: Time your mother got over me and found a new fellow.

LEWIS: I look after her all right.

DEAD DAD: She doesn't like you working for Oscar.

LEWIS: *(To himself.)* I bet she's let the fire go out.

He checks. She has. LEWIS looks about the place.

LEWIS: You know, I think I might say a quick hello to Danny and Hannah.

DEAD DAD: Good idea. Good to talk to people like Danny, who don't own mountains, and to people like Hannah, who aren't whores.

LEWIS: Yeh.

DEAD DAD: Yeh.

LEWIS bolts a wall and goes into DANNY & HANNAH's living room.

DANNY is a frail, unhealthy-looking man in his mid-thirties. HANNAH is strong, dark and attractive. They all sit shivering by a fireplace.

DANNY: I'll get a bit of coal for this fire. Not sure I'll be able to find any, but I'll try.

HANNAH: We've got to have some brightness now and then.

LEWIS: Yes. Brightness is all right.

LEWIS watches DANNY slowly go outside. He takes a jacket from a hook revealing GWYN beneath it, and exits. GWYN watches the following.

LEWIS: How are things, Hannah?

HANNAH: Oh, they're… you know…

LEWIS & GWYN: No. Go on.

HANNAH: Christ Lewis, I get fed up sometimes. So fed up I can't stand it.

LEWIS: You wait, Hannah. You wait til Danny gets work. Things'll be fine.

HANNAH: He had work, Lewis. Last week. Delivering coal for Simon Simons.

We see DANNY, last week, picking up coal sacks. He struggles with various weights. Eventually, one is so heavy he falls backwards.

LEWIS: He has to work up some strength. That's all.

HANNAH: Where the hell from, Lewis?

LEWIS: I don't know, Hannah. There's a lot of things I don't know.

HANNAH: No. But you've got strength.

LEWIS: Life's hard without it.

Enter DANNY with a shovel with a single piece of coal on it.

DANNY: Well, that's the lot, and even that took some finding.

He throws it on the fire. The fire glows a little brighter. He takes his jacket off and hands it to GWYN.

I've had to buy every lump we've burned since Oscar got policemen to stand guard over his tip and put a stop to us helping ourselves.

LEWIS: That's Oscar for you.

DANNY: How do you do it, Lewis? You ought to know different. You got some sort of brain, but you work for Oscar

HANNAH: It's a job, Danny.

DANNY: Your old man would have kicked you over the roof for taking money off such a crap. Yet you help to keep him in the way!

LEWIS: As long as he pays me

DANNY: That's not the point!

HANNAH: That *is* the point, Danny! Let's be glad somebody can have a job and keep it, shall we? So long Lewis. I'm going to bed.

HANNAH exits.

DANNY: That was meant for me, that comment. Last week I got a job –

LEWIS: So I heard. Collapsed on the pavement on top a pile of coal.

DANNY: I've waited years for work to come by and it's finished almost before it started.

LEWIS: That's tough, Danny.

DANNY: But it's not the worst of it.

LEWIS: Oh?

DANNY: The doctor said my heart is bad.

LEWIS: Your heart?

DANNY: Very bad, judging by the solemn look on his face.

LEWIS: Does Hannah know?

DANNY: She'll know soon enough. I was healthy when we got married. And strong. I could've dug a whole mountain away, so long as it was one that didn't belong to some bastard like Oscar.

LEWIS: That's a hell of a thing, Danny.

DANNY: They're cruel bastards, Lewis, these people who stand above us and kick our sorry lives into any shape that pleases. They've beaten me. Sucked me dry as a cork. So there'll be no grand revenge on my behalf… although, I will do one thing… so small it's pathetic but…

GWYN THOMAS: Say "You're not going to pay for any more coal."

DANNY: I'm not going to pay for any more coal. How's that for a wonderful bloody triumph? This is me standing up to defy the world, and how do I defy it? I say I'm not going to pay for any more coal! That's life at its highest, that is, eh?

LEWIS: And where are you going to get your coal?

GWYN THOMAS: Say "From Oscar's tip."

DANNY: From Oscar's tip.

LEWIS: Danny, he'll put you in jail.

DANNY: He can send me to Hell for all I care, but I'll be up there tomorrow morning.

LEWIS: I advise you against all this, Danny. Oscar is savage in his ways with trespassers, especially those who lay their hands on what he thinks belongs to him.

DANNY: See you tomorrow, Lewis.

LEWIS: All right, Danny.

DANNY leaves the house, and sees HANNAH in the top window.

She sings a reprise of "Body And Soul":

SONG: What lies before me
    The future is stormy
    A winter that's grey and old
    Unless there's magic
    The end will be tragic
    And echo the tale that's been told so often

GWYN THOMAS: The Valley bore strange fruit in the form of folk. Some where unusually tall and designed for roofing. Some were born stunted, squat, dark, their physiques perfect for the pits. Others merely affected an air of sadness and looked like something that had grown out the ground…

The path to OSCAR's.

NO DOUBT, dressed in heavy rainproof fishing gear, limps towards LEWIS.

LEWIS: God, it's a lovely morning, No Doubt.

NO DOUBT: Oh, no doubt.

LEWIS: What brings you up here so early, No Doubt?

NO DOUBT: It's my leg, see? It hurts in the morning, so I like to come up here before starting on the tip and stamp a bit of life into it.

LEWIS: What happened?

NO DOUBT: Got a nasty crack from a tumbling stone one month previous.

LEWIS: Sorry to hear that, No Doubt. You be sure you take care of that leg. You'll get no compensation from Oscar.

NO DOUBT: Oh, I wouldn't want any, anyway.

LEWIS: You wouldn't?

NO DOUBT: No. I like Oscar. I wouldn't press the man for compensation.

LEWIS: Hah?

NO DOUBT: I'm very grateful to him.

LEWIS: What the hell for?

NO DOUBT: Giving me the chance to work on his mountain.

LEWIS: You are joking?

NO DOUBT: I feel at home up here. Always so nice and peaceful.

LEWIS: You ought to've been born a sheep, No Doubt.

NO DOUBT: No doubt.

LEWIS: No doubt.

NO DOUBT: Yes?

Explosion!

MR WILSON: The education of the masses will only begin when the desire for beauty is a feature of one and all, Mrs Wilson.

MRS WILSON: Beauty, Mr Wilson? In these Terraces? Good luck to you with that venture!

MR WILSON: We should play opera. On the gramophone. To the customers. And put a stop to those crude, rowdy tunes they bawl.

MRS WILSON: It's difficult enough keeping ourselves alive, let alone listening to opera!

MR WILSON: A dose of beauty wouldn't go amiss on you, my dear.

Explosion!

OSCAR's bedroom.

OSCAR sits in bed and smokes a cigarette.

LEWIS: What's the matter with you, Oscar?

OSCAR stares.

Christ, man. You look like you could use a change. Why not go away for a spell? You could do something different, something you've never done before… Like work.

OSCAR stares at him. Pats the bed. LEWIS doesn't budge. OSCAR pats the bed again.

LEWIS: I'm fine where I am.

OSCAR is about to break into a howling rage.

Alright, alright.

LEWIS sits. OSCAR draws near.

OSCAR: I want… to kill somebody, Lewis.

LEWIS: Kill somebody? What? Just for the hell of it?

OSCAR nods.

LEWIS: And who would you kill, Oscar? One of those poor
bastards out on your tip?

OSCAR chuckles.

LEWIS: Yeh, why not? Their lives aren't worth spit. And you
own 'em. You can do what you want with 'em!

OSCAR gets excited.

They're nothing, right? I mean, if it wasn't for you and
your mountain, they'd be rotting in their beds at home
making more belly-crawling bastards like themselves. Why
should they live, eh? It's not like they've got such a right to
life as a bloody king! Or you!

OSCAR realises he's being made a fool of.

Yes! That's the thing to make you tingle, I bet. Kill
someone! Smash somebody into hell and shout as you're
smashing: "There you are, you poor blundering bastard!
There go your dreams and your eyes and your hopes and
your arms and all the bloody things that make you feel so
grand and proud!"

OSCAR lunges at LEWIS.

OSCAR: Little shit! Don't you forget! You wouldn't be living if
it wasn't for me!

LEWIS: Christ. So even I'd come in handy, wouldn't I? You
could try it out on me, this new desire, and see how it feels.
That would put a stop to my bloody cocky ways!

*Suddenly, OSCAR roars, dives over the side of the bed and produces
a chamber pot. He hurls it at LEWIS.*

GWYN bounces the pot wildly around the room.

So you'd like to kill people, would you, because your
mouth's a bit stale after last night's beer and you're a bit
worn out by women? Take some poor element's life just to

give you a few new thrills? Owning a mountain's driving you off your head, boy.

OSCAR lights another cigarette.

Yeh, that's it. You keep tremblin' and smokin' and owning it all.

LEWIS exits.

SONG: Lord and master!
Oscar! Nothing vaster!
Oscar! In his tower (tower)
Standing tall Mighty power (power)
Lord of All!

The coal tip.

LEWIS stands atop the crumbling mountain of coal, and counts the workers picking below. The clatter and grind of the tipping machine is in the distance.

DEAD DAD: *(Appearing from nowhere.)* What sort of job is this? Counting heads and sacks of coal? Don't you want to get your hands dirty?

LEWIS: What, bent up like those monkeys, getting my guts turned half solid with coal dust? No thanks.

DEAD DAD: Phff! *Counting.*

The tipping machine shudders unhealthily, and comes to a stop.

DEAD DAD: Tipping machine's broken.

LEWIS: I can see that, da'.

OSCAR's kitchen.

LEWIS: Tipper's stopped, Oscar. What do you want me to do?

Tip.

LEWIS: *(To pickers.)* All right! Go home! The lot of you!

NO DOUBT: I don't want to go home, Lewis.

LEWIS: Go on down now, and for Christ's sake don't be so anxious about making such a profit for Oscar.

GWYN THOMAS: *(In NO DOUBT's ear.)* Say "That's not what I'm anxious about."

NO DOUBT: *(As he goes off.)* That's not what I'm anxious about…

LEWIS spots DANNY on the tip with an empty sack over his shoulder. He watches as DANNY stiffly sinks to his knees and starts to pick coal.

LEWIS: What's that daft sod doing?

DEAD DAD: He's doing what he said he was going to do. Collecting his coal.

LEWIS: I know that. It's the fact he's doing it in plain view of Oscar! He'll play hell with Danny if he catches him stealing.

(Shouting, waves his arms.)

Danny? Danny!

DANNY sees through LEWIS and waves.

OSCAR saunters into view and sights set on DANNY. OSCAR approaches DANNY, towering over him.

OSCAR lunges at DANNY. They fight. DANNY gets the better hand, and lifts a rock above OSCAR's head – he throws it to the side. DANNY picks up his sack, continues to pick. OSCAR slowly, slowly, slowly gets himself to his feet.

DANNY, bent low, picks up a piece of coal.

LEWIS watches.

OSCAR turns, a rifle levelled at DANNY.

BOOM!

The shot goes wide. But DANNY's heart goes. As he slowly falls, HANNAH sings.

SONG: I'm lost in the dark
Where is the spark for my love?

I'm lost in the night
Where is the light of my love…?

DANNY lands in a coffin, the lid closes heavily.

OSCAR's kitchen.

LEWIS: Got what you wanted, Oscar? He's dead. How does it feel?

OSCAR is nothing more than a trembling wig now.

OSCAR: Say you didn't see me, Lewis. Say you didn't see me!

LEWIS: I'll say what you want me to say. I got a job with you. The truth's nothing up against that.

OSCAR: That's my boy.

LEWIS: But all the same, he is dead.

OSCAR: Christ! I didn't realise I had such excellent aim!

LEWIS: Your bullet didn't hit him.

OSCAR: No?

LEWIS: He died of fright. He was frightened and he fell. His heart gave out. He thought he'd got away from all this fear. He thought he'd be brave for a change!

OSCAR: What the hell are you talking about? I didn't hit him?

LEWIS: But you fired at him! You stopped his heart.

OSCAR: Say you didn't see me, Lewis.

OSCAR cowers at his feet like a dog. LEWIS kicks him off.

OSCAR: *(Spitting out cash.)* Here. Money.

LEWIS: I don't want it. But I'll take them and say anything you want.

OSCAR: Meg! Food! Thieving bastard. Who was he anyway?

LEWIS: That fellow who's dead out there's a friend of mine. He lived in one of your houses, next door to my mother's, in fact. He never thought much of it. Damp, draughty, bloody hole he said it was. Just like his life. He was a nice chap, Oscar. Quiet.

MEG brings in some food in a bucket.

LEWIS: Enjoy your food. I'd better go and tell whoever ought to be told that somebody's dropped dead on Oscar's tip.

OSCAR's wig sniffs the bucket, jumps in and eats.

Oxford University. Dining Hall.

YOUNG GWYN is squashed between two OXFORD STUDENTS.

OXFORD STUDENT 1: *(To OXFORD STUDENT 2.)* Enjoying your lunch?

OXFORD STUDENT 2: There seems to be something in mine. A small Welsh creature.

OXFORD STUDENT 1: I should complain to the kitchens. Lumps in your soup.

OXFORD STUDENT 2: Let's take a closer look!

They study YOUNG GWYN at close range.

GWYN THOMAS: My time at Oxford University was not a happy one. Had I been a Martian I would not have made smaller contact to the place.

OXFORD STUDENT 1: Such a squat and stunted thing.

YOUNG GWYN: Well, in the valley the average height is 5ft 6. History had meant us to be short, see?

OXFORD STUDENT 2: Didn't I read somewhere that the Welsh stock had been heavily watered down by infusions of Jewish and Negro blood?

YOUNG GWYN: Indeed it has! And proud of it we are, too! You can shake me if you like, just to hear the glug of tainted plasm.

OXFORD STUDENT 1 & 2: Oh?

They examine YOUNG GWYN further.

OXFORD STUDENT 1: What a truly queer specimen.

OXFORD STUDENT 2: Do you think he's in the right place?

YOUNG GWYN/GWYN THOMAS: No. I'm not. And these meals are not for me!

YOUNG GWYN pushes his food away and leaves.

The Back Room of The Harp.

OSCAR reads a newspaper, chuckling at his victory. LEWIS stands by, disgusted.

OSCAR: Ha! There it is, boy! In black and white! The court's verdict: Death by natural causes!

LEWIS: Congratulations, Oscar.

OSCAR: *(Reading.)* "Called forth to testify was Lewis, Oscar's boy, who said – "

LEWIS: *(To court.)* I'd been standing about a hundred yards from the tip when I saw Danny picking. I heard him shout out in pain, saw him come tumbling down. I ran to him… but there was no sign of life.

OSCAR laughs.

OSCAR: *(Reading.)* "Hannah, the wife of the deceased, testified – "

HANNAH sings to the court.

SONG: My life revolved around him
What earthly good am I without him?
My castles have crumbled
But I am his body and –

HANNAH falters.

OSCAR: Christ, Lewis. She was lovely. Boy, she was a pippin!

LEWIS: Who?

OSCAR: That woman in the court we saw.

LEWIS: Oh. You mean Hannah. Aye. She's all right.

OSCAR: I watched her leave. Saw her catch a bus! And catching it in such a lovely way! Oh! I love buses.

LEWIS: You hate buses, Oscar.

OSCAR: I'd give a lot to have her, Lewis. I'd take that sad look off her face. And by the time I've had her, she'd be glad I frightened the guts out of her old man and made him drop down dead!

Enter CLARISSE, with a plate of meat.

CLARISSE: Here's your bacon, liver and kidneys, gentlemen.

As she places the plate, she rubs her leg on LEWIS's thigh. She and LEWIS share a look. Then she collects the empties, rubs her leg on OSCAR's thigh. LEWIS sees this. CLARISSE goes. OSCAR eats meat, drinks and sweats.

OSCAR: I've got to have that woman, Lew. But how the hell'm I going to get her?

GWYN whispers in LEWIS's ear.

LEWIS: I'll get her for you, Oscar.

OSCAR: Don't joke with me or I'll shove your face in that gas fire, I swear I will!

LEWIS: Of course I can get her for you. She'd be keen as hell to get with a man like you. There isn't a woman in the Terraces wouldn't pawn her penniless husband for the likes of Oscar. They're so poor, they got no option. And you own the house she lives in.

OSCAR: I do! I own the bloody house! I own the tip! I own the mountain!

LEWIS: You'd be like a God to her.

OSCAR: A God?

LEWIS: Just like a god. Leave it to me, Oscar. I'll get her for you.

OSCAR: Honest?

LEWIS: I'll bring her to you on a lead. She'll be eating out of your hand before you know it.

The congregation sing.

SONG: Hallelujah!
Hallelujah!
Hallelujah!

HANNAH's House.

HANNAH stares into the fire. DANNY's body is in a cheap, open casket propped up on trestles at the back.

LEWIS: Sorry about Danny. We'll miss him.

HANNAH: Not as much as me.

LEWIS: No. Not as much as you, Hannah.

HANNAH: He never did any harm to all. He just got harm like he always said. He was so patient and kind it withered all the strength out of him. For years I could see the strength going out of him. He wouldn't even give me love in the nights cus he said he wasn't fit to love any woman. He said when things were better it would be different.

God, how we used to pray. I wanted him to love me like he did at the beginning. But always he said not til things are better. We waited too long, Lewis. We waited too long. Christ, I'm sick, Lewis. Sick of being alive like this. I'd rather be like Danny is than sick like this…

LEWIS: Don't talk like that, Hannah.

HANNAH: Forgive me, Lew. I'm so tired. I'll be all right now.

LEWIS: We put up with a lot.

HANNAH: Too much.

LEWIS: We are stepped on.

HANNAH: They stepped on Danny good and proper.

LEWIS: And he never got the chance to get his own back.

HANNAH: No. He was always the one being stepped on.

LEWIS: We ought to step on Oscar.

HANNAH: Who could get high enough to step on him?

GWYN THOMAS: *(In LEWIS's ear.)* Say "You could".

LEWIS: You could.

HANNAH: Me?

LEWIS: Listen, Hannah. Oscar killed Danny.

HANNAH: Don't be daft, Lewis. Things are bad enough.

LEWIS: I was there. I was there when Oscar shot his gun. The bullet came right close to Danny. He was frightened, and he fell.

HANNAH: You told the court how you saw Danny die. You didn't mention anything about Oscar and his gun.

LEWIS: Oscar would have said I was lying. The day Danny died, Oscar said he ought to be allowed to kill a few people, people who were poor, of no account, like Danny. Said it would give him a new feeling. That's why he shot the gun at Danny.

HANNAH: He said all those things?

LEWIS: All those things. He thinks he's a bloody god up there on his mountain.

HANNAH: Said he'd like to kill somebody?

LEWIS: That's it.

HANNAH: Somebody poor, of no account -

LEWIS: That right.

HANNAH: Who wouldn't be missed, by Christ? He said that, did he? Perhaps he won't be missed once I'm done with him!

LEWIS: What are you going to do, Hannah?

GWYN THOMAS: Say "You're going to kill that bastard of an Oscar."

HANNAH: I'm going to kill that bastard of an Oscar.

Explosion!

MR WILSON: The world has gone to hell, Mrs Wilson!

MRS WILSON: What's wrong with that, Mr Wilson?

MR WILSON: I'm talking about the fundamental lack of moral sense.

MRS WILSON: The only use for moral sense in this place is to stuff the chairs with it!

Explosion!

LEWIS: If anyone's got the right to do it, Hannah, it's you.

HANNAH: And I won't do it to get any new feeling, either.

LEWIS: How will you do it?

HANNAH: Get him near me. That's all. Just get him near me.

LEWIS: I can do that, Hannah. He comes when I whistle.

HANNAH: The last thing Danny ever gave me was a hammer.

LEWIS: Oh?

HANNAH: Said he wanted to give me something. So he stole a bloody brand new hammer from the woodwork class down in the Settlement, but he was sorry he did it as soon as he brought it home.

LEWIS: That's Danny, all right.

HANNAH: He hid it away in the drawer, never used it at all, in case anybody would ever see it.

GWYN hands her a hammer.

LEWIS: I'll get him here for you, Hannah.

HANNAH: When?

LEWIS: Tonight.

HANNAH: That's soon.

LEWIS: Oh. Oh, I see. You were just talking. You're not actually meaning what you say. Good night, Hannah.

HANNAH: No. No. I'm not just talking. I could do it even now as I'm standing here. Bring him to me tonight. Tomorrow is the funeral. So Danny'll know he's quits with Oscar before he leaves.

LEWIS: Danny needs some cheering up, God knows. Oscar fancies you, Hannah. And if you can make an eye at him he'll roll all over you.

HANNAH: Buy me some whiskey, will you?

LEWIS: You'll have it.

HANNAH: God, it's quiet in this house.

LEWIS: It is, too.

SONG: Hallelujah!
Hallelujah!

GWYN THOMAS: So, to re-cap: Lewis brings Oscar to Hannah. Hannah's got the hammer. But what should happen next? Do we need another surprise?

GWYN thinks. Behind him, sheep bleat noisily.

GWYN THOMAS: One at a time please!

A sheep bleats.

GWYN THOMAS: We did that in "Simeon". Come on. Let's have some originality here!

Bleats.

GWYN THOMAS: Ewe. Say that again?

Bleats again.

GWYN THOMAS: You little woolly genius! That's brilliant!

HANNAH's.

HANNAH is on the sofa.

LEWIS: She's in there waiting, Oscar. Go on, boy.

(To himself.)

Go get what's coming for you!

DANNY sits up in his coffin, climbs out, opens the curtains revealing LEWIS, GWYN THOMAS and LEWIS's DEAD DAD. They exchange a look, and watch on…

HANNAH's arm starts to stretch out across the sofa toward the cushion.

LEWIS: She's reaching for it… reaching… reach! Reach for the hammer!

The people of the Terraces chant as HANNAH attempts to murder OSCAR, then (to LEWIS's horror) gives herself to him.

CHORUS: Huh… (x8.)

Reach! (huh) Reach! (huh) Reach for the hammer hannah Reach for the hammer hannah Reach for the hammer (huh huh) Reach for the hammer Bring the tool to him (huh)

Bring it home and brain him Crack his skull and break him Smack it (smack it) Crack it (crack it) Open to the brains (huh)

Swing it (swing it) Bring it (bring it) Down so hard (so hard)

Drive it in (so hard) So hard Slam it down (down) Down! (slam) Down! (wham)

Reach (huh) Reach (huh) Reach for the hammer hannah Bring the tool to him (huh)

Bring the hammer down (huh) Bring the hammer down (huh) Hit it (hit it)
Split it (split it)
Open to the brains
Hit his head (hit his head) Til he's dead (so dead) Smash it down So hard! So hard! Stick it in! So deep! So deep! Slam it down (down) Down! (slam) Down! (wham)
Reach (huh) Reach (huh) Reach for the hammer hannah Reach for the hammer Bring the tool to

him Hammer (hannah) Hammer (hannah) Hannah
(hammer) Hannah (hammer) Hit him (hannah) Hannah
(hit him) Hard (so hard) Hit him *Hard*

Hallelujah (hit him) Halleujah (hard) Hannah (hard)
Hannah (Hallelujah) Hit him (Hallelujah)
Hard (Hannah) Hard (Hannah) Hit Him
(Hallelujah) *Hard*

Hit Him (Hard) Hannah Hit Him (Hard) Hannah
(Hallelujah)

Hit Him (Hard) Hannah Hit Him (Hard)
Hannah (Hit Him) *Hard*

Hit Him (Hannah) x3 *Hard*

Hit Him (Hit Him) x8

HANNAH HA! (x12.)

HANNAH!

*It is over. DANNY looks at LEWIS, then sadly returns to his coffin.
DEAD DAD retreats into shadow.*

OSCAR: I'm done. Take me home. Lead the way. Oh, she's
mine, boy. Like this mountain mine's, and the coal tip
and the dumb elements picking the stuff! The Terraces are
mine! And the trees and the wind and this jacket and these
hands and you Lewis and the sky –

SONG: Violator - Oscar!
Revelator - Oscar!
Righteous judgement (judgement.)
Kingdom come!
Vengeful servant (servant)
See it done!

*LEWIS grabs OSCAR violently and drags him up the mountain once
more.*

OSCAR tumbles over the edge and plummets into the quarry below.

OSCAR: Noooooooooooooooooooooooooo!!!!!!!

HANNAH's.

She is lying on her side, head on the cushion.

The "Parkinson" theme tune begins.

PARKY: I was going to ask you, Hannah, and correct me if I'm wrong but, weren't you supposed to kill Oscar with a hammer?

HANNAH: I was going to do it. Honest. I was!

She flings the cushion away to reveal the hammer.

PARKY: But you didn't because…?

HANNAH: I didn't know… I didn't know who he was… when he came in I thought… I thought he was Danny…

PARKY: We all saw the scene. Heard the chanting. Quite extraordinary. It begs the question: why give yourself to him so easily?

HANNAH: I've been so cold… so cold for so long…

PARKY: Ladies and gentlemen – Hannah.

LEWIS hands her the bottle of whiskey.

LEWIS: Drink that, or you'll go mad, Hannah, and me with you.

She drinks it like water.

You are lovely, Hannah. You are.

She sits on the sofa, staring out. LEWIS goes to DANNY's coffin.

LEWIS: You're lucky, boy, Danny. There's a peculiar bunch performing round here.

LEWIS walks out of the house without looking to HANNAH.

GWYN THOMAS appears reading a newspaper.

GWYN THOMAS: "The works of Gwyn Thomas are unique and are sure to survive him for many decades to come."

(Improvised every night but for now it's…)

The Prestatyn Bugle.

LEWIS walks by.

LEWIS: Mother? Mother!

GWYN THOMAS: Hello, Lewis.

LEWIS: Who are you?

GWYN THOMAS: I'm Gwyn Thomas.

LEWIS: Never heard of ya.

The people of the Terraces appear from their doors.

GWYN THOMAS: I wanted to say to you, to all of you, please do not regard any serious conception of yourself as having any truly valid meaning. We're all, all of us, the victims of a great over-riding joke.

GWYN'S FATHER: There's little wrong with that!

GWYN THOMAS: As my father used to say.

GWYN'S FATHER: So long as it's a damned good one. Gwyn? Gwyn!

GWYN THOMAS: Yes, dad?

GWYN's FATHER goes to YOUNG GWYN and hands him the urn.

GWYN'S FATHER: I won't be long. Drink your lemonade. And don't get dark thoughts.

They start to hum "All Through The Night".

Somewhere in the Terraces, an old television crackles to life and shows the real GWYN THOMAS on "PARKINSON" doing what he does best.

GWYN THOMAS is delighted he's on telly.

GWYN THOMAS: *(Re: telly.)* That's me, that is!

YOUNG GWYN passes the urn along the people of the Terraces. As each character receives the urn they are touched with a strange warmth.

SONG: Love, to thee my thoughts are turning
All through the night

71

All for thee my heart is yearning
All through the night
Though sad fate our lives may sever
Parting will not last forever
There's a hope that leaves me never
All through the night
All through the night
All through the night
Though our hearts are wrapped in sorrow
There's a promise of tomorrow
All through the night!

GWYN THOMAS darts in and out of the congregation, delighting in the fact that it's him in the urn.

GWYN THOMAS: *(Re: urn.)* That's me, that is!

SONG: *(Gentle.)*

All through the night
My love let peace attend thee
All through the night
Through the night
Through the night
Through the night
All through… the… night…

GWYN THOMAS: It's all a joke. One great, sad, beautiful joke!

GWYN THOMAS, our GWYN, chuckles to himself.

END.